A
Book
of
Comfort

THE HELEN STEINER RICE FOUNDATION

> God knows no strangers, He loves us all,
> The poor, the rich, the great, the small.
> He is a Friend who is always there
> To share our troubles and lessen our care.
> No one is a stranger in God's sight,
> For God is love and in His light
> May we, too, try in our small way
> To make new friends from day to day.

Whatever the celebration, whatever the day, whatever the event, whatever the occasion, Helen Steiner Rice possessed the ability to express the appropriate feeling for that particular moment in time.

A happening became happier, a sentiment more sentimental, a memory more memorable because of her deep sensitivity to put into understandable language the emotion being experienced. Her positive attitude, her concern for others, and her love of God are identifiable threads woven into her life, her work . . . and even her death.

Prior to her passing, she established the HELEN STEINER RICE FOUNDATION, a nonprofit corporation whose purpose is to award grants to worthy charitable programs that aid the elderly, the needy, and the poor. In her lifetime, these were the individuals about whom Mrs. Rice was greatly concerned.

Royalties from the sale of this book will add to the financial capabilities of the HELEN STEINER RICE FOUNDATION, thus making possible additional grants to various qualified, worthwhile, and charitable programs. Because of her foresight, her caring, and her deep convictions, Helen Steiner Rice continues to touch a countless number of lives. Thank you for your assistance in helping to keep Helen's dream alive.

Virginia J. Ruehlmann, Administrator
The Helen Steiner Rice Foundation
Suite 2100, Atrium Two
221 E. Fourth Street
Cincinnati, Ohio 45201

Helen Steiner Rice

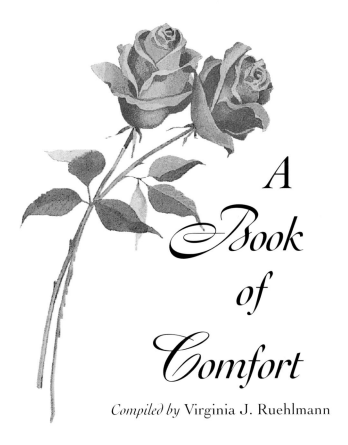

A

Book

of

Comfort

Compiled by Virginia J. Ruehlmann

HUTCHINSON
LONDON

© Virginia J. Ruehlmann and The Helen Steiner Rice Foundation 1995

Illustrations by Jack Brouwer

The right of Helen Steiner Rice to be identified as Author of this work has been asserted by Helen Steiner Rice in accordance with the Copyright, Designs and Patents Act, 1988

First published in the United States in 1994 by Fleming H. Revell

This edition first published in 1995 by Hutchinson

Random House UK Ltd
20 Vauxhall Bridge Road, London SW1V 2SA

Random House Australia (Pty) Ltd
20 Alfred Street, Milsons Point, Sydney, NSW 2061, Australia

Random House New Zealand Ltd
18 Poland Road, Glenfield, Auckland 10, New Zealand

Random House South Africa (Pty) Ltd
PO Box 337, Bergvlei, 2012, South Africa

A CIP catalogue record for this book is available from the British Library

Printed and bound by Tien Wah Press in Singapore

ISBN 0 09 1792320

Unless otherwise noted, Scripture quotations are taken from the Revised Version of the Bible, copyright 1946, 1952, 1971, and 1973 by the Division of Christian Education of the National Council of the Churches of Christ in the United States of America.

Scripture verses marked NAB are taken from the New American Standard Bible, © the Lockman Foundation 1960, 1962, 1963, 1968, 1971, 1972, 1973, 1975, 1977.

Scripture verses marked NIV are taken from the HOLY BIBLE: NEW INTERNATIONAL VERSION ®. NIV ®. Copyright © 1973, 1978, 1984 by International Bible Society. Used by permission of Zondervan Publishing House.

Dedicated
to those individuals
who are in need of comfort
and
to those who extend it

Contents

God Knows Best

God only sends us sadness
    and the agony of sorrow
To help our ever-restless souls
    to grow to meet tomorrow . . .
May you find much comfort,
    and may you also be blessed,
When you read the contents of this book,
    remembering that God knows best.

Be strong and of good courage, do not fear or be in dread of them:
for it is the Lord your God who goes with you: he will not fail you
or forsake you.

Deuteronomy 31:6

Introduction

At the passing of a loved one, those left behind feel a profound sense of sorrow. Pangs of deep loneliness set in as the survivors envision a future without the deceased. No longer will the loved one be present physically to share conversations, walks, hugs, ideas, but it's important to realize that departed loved ones do live on in our hearts, in memories of their teachings, and in the lives of all who knew them. While death brings sadness, there should also be a sense of joy as the loved one enters into the home of our Father.

When grieving occurs, the use of available resources for positive coping are mandatory. Helen Steiner Rice experienced several seemingly devastating tragedies in her life, but she adjusted and rebounded by applying teachings found in the Scriptures.

Many of her inspirational poems are based on passages from the Bible. She was adamant in crediting her strength and her talent to God. She used His gifts to express in verse and prose what she had learned. These are shared with you in the following pages.

It is the ability to understand, to apply, to trust, and to live by the lessons found in the Scriptures that will sustain each person on the journey through periods of sorrow. It is my heartfelt wish that by reading this collection you will be afforded personal comfort and assisted in the art of comforting others.

Eternally,
Virginia J. Ruehlmann

Comfort, comfort my people, says your God.
                    Isaiah 40:1

Through the Deep Valleys

I know the loneliness you are experiencing, but after the first stabbing anguish of grief has been softened by time, you will find great comfort in knowing that our dear ones are safe and free from all tears, trials, troubles, and temptations, for now they are where nothing can ever hurt them again.

I have always felt at times like this there is so little anyone can say. In a death we find that we are drawn closer to one another and to God, and heaven seems a little nearer, God's promise a little clearer, and His love a little dearer.

I am trying to say that in the kingdom of the Lord there is nothing lost forever. If we believe God's promise, we will meet all those who left us and be together in His kingdom forever.

H.S.R.

Thy kingdom is an everlasting kingdom, and thy dominion endures throughout all generations.

Psalm 145:13

Things We Cannot Understand

There are many things in life
    that we cannot understand,
But we must trust God's judgment
    and be guided by His hand,
And all who have God's blessings
    can rest safely in His care,
For He promises safe passage
    on the wings of faith and prayer!

However, as it is written: "No eye has seen, no ear has heard, no mind conceived what God has prepared for those who love him" — but God has revealed it to us by his Spirit.

1 Corinthians 2:9–10 NIV

God Is Beside You

Our Father in heaven
  always knows what is best,
And if you trust in His wisdom,
  your life will be blessed . . .
For always remember that,
  whatever betide you,
You are never alone,
  for God is beside you.

I will turn their mourning into gladness;
I will give them comfort and joy instead of sorrow.
  Jeremiah 31:13 NIV

Our Refuge and Our Strength

The Lord is our salvation
    and our strength in every fight,
Our Redeemer and protector
    our eternal guiding light . . .
He has promised to sustain us,
    He's our refuge from all harms,
And He holds us all securely
    in His everlasting arms!

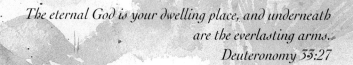

The eternal God is your dwelling place, and underneath
are the everlasting arms.
Deuteronomy 33:27

Secure in His Love

Just close your eyes
  and open your heart
And feel your worries
  and cares depart . . .
Yield yourself
  to the Father above
And let Him hold you
  secure in His love.
For He hears every prayer
  and answers each one
When we pray in His name,
  "Thy will be done,"
And the burdens that seemed
  too heavy to bear
Are lifted away
  on the wings of prayer.

Pray then like this: Our Father who art in heaven, hallowed be thy name. Thy kingdom come, Thy will be done, on earth as it is in heaven.

Matthew 6:9–10

The Clouds of Today

There is always hope of tomorrow
 to brighten the clouds of today . . .
There is always a corner for turning,
 no matter how weary the way . . .
So just look ahead to tomorrow
 and trust that you'll find waiting there
The sunlight that seemed to be hidden
 by yesterday's clouds of despair.

There is never a cloud the sun doesn't shine through.

H.S.R.

Comfort

Although it sometimes seems to us
 our prayers have not been heard,
God always knows our every need
 without a single word.
And He will not forsake us
 even though the way seems steep,
For always He is near to us,
 a tender watch to keep.
And in good time, He'll answer us,
 and in His love He'll send
Greater things than we have asked
 and blessings without end.
So though we do not understand
 why trouble comes to man,
Can we not be contented
 just to know that it's God's plan?

I lift my eyes to the hills. From whence does my help come? My help comes from the Lord, who made heaven and earth. He will not let your foot be moved, he who keeps you will not slumber.

Psalm 121:1–3

Let Not Your Heart Be Troubled

Whenever I am troubled
    and lost in deep despair,
I bundle all my troubles up
    and go to God in prayer . . .
I tell Him I am heartsick
    and lost and lonely, too,
That my mind is deeply burdened
    and I don't know what to do . . .
But I know He stilled the tempest
    and calmed the angry sea,
And I humbly ask if, in His love,
    He'll do the same for me . . .
And then I just keep quiet
    and think only thoughts of peace,
And as I abide in stillness
    my restless murmurings cease.

And behold, there arose a great storm on the sea, so that the boat was being swamped by the waves; but he was asleep. And they went and woke him, saying, "Save us Lord; we are perishing." Then he rose and rebuked the winds and the sea; and there was a great calm.

Matthew 8:24–27

In Him We Live and Move and Have Our Being

We walk in a world that is strange and unknown
   and in the midst of the crowd we still feel alone.
We question our purpose, our part, and our place,
   in this land of mystery suspended in space.
We probe and explore and try hard to explain
   the tumult of thoughts that our minds entertain . . .
But all of our probings and complex explanations
   of man's inner feelings and fears and frustrations
Still leave us engulfed in the mystery of life
   with all of its struggles and suffering and strife,
Unable to fathom what tomorrow will bring,
   but there is one truth to which we can cling,
For while life's a mystery man can't understand
   the great giver of life is holding our hand,
And safe in His care there is no need for seeing.
   for in Him we live and move and have our being.

We live by faith, not by sight.
2 Corinthians 5:7 NIV

"*I Am the Way, the Truth, and the Life*"

I am the way,
  so just follow Me
Though the way be rough
  and you cannot see.
I am the truth
    which all men seek,
So heed not false prophets
  nor the words that they speak.
I am the life,
  and I hold the key
That opens the door
  to eternity.
And in this dark world,
  I am the light
To a Promised Land
  where there is no night.

Thomas said to him, "Lord, we do not know where you are going; how can we know the way?" Jesus said to him, "I am the way, and the truth, and the life; no one comes to the Father, but by me."

John 14:5–7

The Comfort and Sweetness of Peace

After the clouds, the sunshine,
  after the winter, the spring,
After the shower, the rainbow,
  for life is a changeable thing.
After the night, the morning,
  bidding all darkness cease,
After life's cares and sorrows,
  the comfort and sweetness of peace.

Sing for joy, O heavens, and exult, O earth; break forth, O mountains, into singing! For the Lord has comforted his people, and will have compassion on his afflicted.

Isaiah 49:13

God Holds the Key

God in His goodness has promised
    that the cross He gives us to wear
Will never exceed our endurance
    or be more than our strength can bear . . .
And secure in that blessed assurance,
    we can smile as we face tomorrow,
For God holds the key to the future,
    and no sorrow or care need we borrow!

Every mile we walk in sorrow brings us nearer to God's tomorrow!

H.S.R.

For everything there is a season, and a time for every matter under heaven: a time to be born, and a time to die.

Ecclesiastes 3:1–2

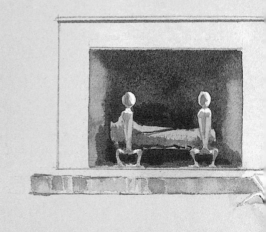

Passing of a Parent

Our lives are so uncertain, unsure, and unfathomable, and God alone knows the pattern of our days.

It is difficult to realize that your mother is no longer here with us, and yet she is so close to us in spirit, having only gone beyond the sound of our voices and the touch of our hands.

I wanted to talk with you, but there were many things that made it impossible, and I knew my words would be a poor substitute for a loving heart which silently reaches out to say, "I care!"

Feeling about death the way I do and knowing death opens the door to life evermore, I cannot help but feel that God especially loved your mother to have so gently lifted her over the threshold into life everlasting. The sadness of her death is softened in knowing that she never had to linger in the twilight of life and become incapacitated and unable to be her own sweet, active, cheerful self. How wonderful to know that with one swift, little step she crossed the threshold of eternity.

Death is always a sobering experience, but in the hands of God, it, too, becomes a time for rejoicing.

In the heavenly home above, mothers wait to welcome those they love.

H.S.R.

Face to Face

All who believe
   in God's mercy and grace
Will meet their loved ones
   face to face
Where time is endless
   and joy unbroken
And only the words
   of God's love are spoken.

For this we declare to you by the word of the Lord, that we who are alive, who are left until the coming of the Lord, shall not precede those who have fallen asleep. For the Lord himself will descend from heaven with a cry of command, with the archangel's call, and with the sound of the trumpet of God. And the dead in Christ will rise first; then we who are alive, who are left, shall be caught up together with them in the clouds to meet the Lord in the air; and so we shall always be with the Lord. Therefore comfort one another with these words.

1 Thessalonians 4:15–18

On the Other Side of Death

Death is a gateway
   we all must pass through
To reach the fair land
   where the soul's born anew,
For man's born to die,
   and his sojourn on earth
Is a short span of years
   beginning with birth.
And like Pilgrims we wander,
   until death takes our hand,
And we start on the journey
   to God's Promised Land—
A place where we'll find
   no suffering or tears,
Where time is not counted
   in days, months, or years—
And in that fair city
   that God has prepared
Are unending joys
   to be happily shared
With all of our loved ones
   who patiently wait
On death's other side
   to open the gate.

Life Is Eternal

"Life is eternal," the good Lord said,
    so do not think of your loved one as dead
For death is only a stepping-stone
    to a beautiful life we have never known,
A place where God promised man he would be
    eternally happy and safe and free,
A wonderful land where we live anew
    when our journey on earth is over and through.
So trust God and doubt Him never,
    for all who love Him live forever,
And while we cannot understand
    just let the Savior take your hand,
For when death's angel comes to call
    God is so great and we're so small . . .
And there is nothing you need fear
    for faith in God makes all things clear.

*Life is eternal and love is immortal, and death is a gateway—an
entrance and portal—into a life that no man can envision, for
God has a greater perspective and vision.*

H.S.R.

Since Mother Went Away

Since Mother went away,
    it seems she's nearer than before,
I cannot touch her hand,
    and yet she's with me more and more,
And the years have never lessened
    the longing in my heart
That came the day I realized
    that we must dwell apart,
And just as long as memory lives,
    my mother cannot die,
For in my heart she's living still
    as passing years go by.

God had need for a special angel, so He called your dear mother above, but she's only as far away as your hearts, and she lives as before in your love.

H.S.R.

She Will Always Be Near

Words cannot soften your sorrow
   or lessen your sadness today,
But may you find comfort and solace
   as time goes along its way,
For the love of a wonderful mother
   lives on in the heart through each year,
And death cannot mean that you've lost her
   for in memory she'll always be near.

Words are a poor substitute for a loving heart which silently reaches out from time to time just to say, "I care and I think of you!" But it seems our days in this world are not fashioned so that we can always do the things we most want.

H.S.R.

When I Must Leave You

When I must leave you for a little while,
  please do not grieve and shed wild tears
And hug your sorrow to you through the years,
  but start out bravely with a smile
And for my sake and in my name,
  live on and do all the things the same.
Feed not your loneliness on empty days,
  but fill each waking hour in useful ways.
Reach out your hand in comfort and in cheer,
  and I, in turn, will comfort you and hold you near.
And never, never be afraid to die,
  for I am waiting for you in the sky.

Jesus said to her, "I am the resurrection and the life; he who believes in me, though he die, yet shall he live, and whoever lives and believes in me shall never die. Do you believe this?"

John 11:25–26

"Come to me, all who labor and are heavy laden, and I will give you rest. Take my yoke upon you, and learn from me; for I am gentle and lowly in heart, and you will find rest for your souls. For my yoke is easy, and my burden is light."

Matthew 11:28–30

Sympathy on the Death of a Spouse

If we never suffered tragedy, and we never felt sorrow, how could our souls grow? In my husband's tragic death, it was difficult for me, when I was young, to see what the purpose could have been. But now I know that he sacrificed his life that my life might be lived in a fuller and richer way, for his sudden death transformed my entire life. I could never have done what I am doing now if I had not felt the pangs of sorrow, for you cannot dry the tears of those who weep unless you have cried yourself.

I know, when death comes flashing out of a bright sky suddenly and unexpectedly in the midst of youthful enjoyment when life is flushed with hope and filled with dreams, it is very, very difficult to accept God's judgment. It is hard to reconcile ourselves to such a loss when God asks us to give up someone young and in mid-career with abundant years stretching ahead of them, for to have a life so suddenly silenced is beyond our understanding.

May God comfort you and show you the way. Remember, God does not comfort us to make us more comfortable. He comforts us so that we may also become comforters.

Words say so little when the heart means so much.

H.S.R.

Your sun shall no more go down, nor your moon withdraw itself; for the Lord will be your everlasting light, and your days of mourning shall be ended.

Isaiah 60:20

Your Heart Is Heavy

Today your heart is heavy
   with sorrow and grief,
But as days turn to months
   may you find sweet relief
In knowing your loved one
   is not far away,
But is with you in spirit
   every hour of the day.

Only through great suffering can we really come to know what God is really like, and inner strength comes from facing trouble and suffering and enduring it.

H.S.R.

Waiting at Eternity's Door

Death beckoned him with outstretched hand
   and whispered softly of an unknown land.
He took death's hand without a fear,
   For God, who brought him safely here,
Had promised He would lead the way
   into eternity's bright day.
For none of us need go alone
   into the valley that's unknown,
But guided by our Father's hand
   we journey to the Promised Land . . .
And as his loving, faithful wife,
   who shared his home and heart and life,
You will find comfort for your grief
   in knowing death brought sweet relief.
For now he is free from all suffering and pain,
   and your great loss became his gain.
You know his love is with you still,
   for he loved you in life and always will,

For love like yours can never end
  because it is the perfect blend
Of joys and sorrows, smiles and tears
  that just grows stronger through the years.
So think of your loved one as living above,
  no farther away than your undying love,
And now he is happy and free once more,
  and he waits for you at eternity's door.

May You Find Comfort

May you find comfort in the thought
  that sorrow, grief, and woe
Are sent into our lives sometimes
  to help our souls to grow.
For through the depths of sorrow,
  comes understanding love,
And peace and truth and comfort
  are sent from God above.

Listen With Your Heart

Memories are treasures
   time cannot take away,
So may you be surrounded
   by happy ones today.
May all the love and tenderness
   of golden years well spent
Come back today to fill your heart
   with beauty and content,
And may you walk down memory lane
   and meet the one you love,
For while you cannot see him,
   he'll be watching from above . . .
So for his sake be happy
   and show him that his love
Has proven strong and big enough
   to reach down from above.

*For just as the Father raises the dead and gives them life, even so
the Son gives life to whom he is pleased to give it.*

                                      John 5:21 NIV

There Are No Words

There are no words; what can I say?
At last her sweet soul winged its way
To peace and freedom in the sky
Where never again will she suffer or cry.
It's all a part of God's great plan
Which remains a mystery to man.
We cannot understand His ways
Nor can we count our earthly days,
But who are we to question and doubt?
God knoweth well what He's about;
He knew she longed to go to sleep
Where only angels, a vigil keep.
The pain of living grew too great
No longer could she stay and wait.
She did not want to leave her special dear,
But she had finished her work down here.
So she closed her eyes and when she awoke,
These are the words the Master spoke . . .
"Welcome, my child, you are home at last,
And now the burden of living is past."
So weep not, she has just gone ahead,
Don't think of her as being dead.
She's out of sight for a little while,
And you'll miss her touch and her smile,

But you know she is safe in the home above
Where there is nothing but peace and love.
And, surely, you would not deny her peace . . .
And you're glad that she has found release.
Think of her there as a soul that is free,
And home at last, where she wanted to be.

As Long As You Live and Remember, Your Loved One Lives in Your Heart!

May tender memories
  soften your grief,
May fond recollection
  bring you relief,
And may you find comfort
  and peace in the thought
Of the joy that knowing
  your loved one brought.
For time and space
  can never divide
Or keep your loved one
  from your side
When memory paints
  in colors true
The happy hours
  that belonged to you.

*May it comfort you to know your loved one
has just gone away out of a restless, careworn
world into a brighter day.*

H.S.R.

In the Hands of God, Even Death Is a Time for Rejoicing

When death brings weeping
    and the heart is filled with sorrow,
It calls us to seek God
    as we ask about tomorrow.
And in these hours of heart-hurt,
    we draw closer to believing
That even death, in God's hands,
    is not a time for grieving
But a time for joy in knowing
    death is just a stepping-stone
To a life that's everlasting,
    such as we have never known.

And I heard a loud voice from the throne saying, "Now the dwelling of God is with men, and he will live with them. They will be his people, and God himself will be with them and be their God. He will wipe every tear from their eyes. There will be no more death or mourning or crying or pain, for the old order of things has passed away."

Revelation 21:3–4 NIV

"Let not your hearts be troubled; believe in God, believe also in me. In my Father's house are many rooms; if it were not so, would I have told you that I go to prepare a place for you? And when I go and prepare a place for you, I will come again and will take you to myself, that where I am you may be also."

John 14:1–3

Consolation on the Loss of a Child

In the early days of our great country, a father and his young son were making a journey into the nearby village to acquire some tools and supplies. Starting early in the morning, the two set forth on their assignment. To reach their destination, they had to cross a narrow stream and proceed through the woods, the countryside, and finally into the center of town.

After completing their mission, they began their return trip home. As they walked along, a severe thunderstorm erupted. With the heavy downpour of water, the stream that was virtually nonexistent in the morning swelled to twice its size, and the waters swirled viciously against tree roots and rocks and rolled furiously downstream.

Fear rose within the child and the wise father offered to carry his son. Into the open arms of the father climbed the youngster, and experiencing safety and security, he quickly fell asleep in his father's strong and protective arms.

On arriving home the father placed the sleeping child into bed. In the morning with the sun shining at the windows, the youngster awoke in pleasant and comfortable surroundings. Safe, comfortable and content, no longer fearful, he inquired, "Am I home? Did my father carry me across the raging waters?" His mother responded with, "Yes, my child, your father brought you safely home. You are in your room in your father's house, snug and unharmed."

So it will be with each of us as we cross "the river" and awaken in a special room in a very special house.

The Tiny Rosebud God Picked to Bloom in Heaven

The Master Gardener
  from heaven above
Planted a seed
  in the garden of love,
And from it there grew
  a rosebud small
That never had time
  to open at all.
For God in His perfect
  and all-wise way
Chose this rose
  for His heavenly bouquet,
And great was the joy
  of this tiny rose
To be the one our Father chose
  to leave earth's garden
For one on high
  where roses bloom always
And never die.

So, while you can't see
   your precious rose bloom,
You know the great Gardener
   from the upper room
Is watching and tending
   this wee rose with care,
Tenderly touching
   each petal so fair.
So think of your darling
   with the angels above,
Secure and contented
   and surrounded by love,
And remember God blessed
   and enriched your lives, too,
For in dying your darling
   brought heaven closer to you!

God Needed an Angel in Heaven

When Jesus lived upon the earth
   so many years ago,
He called the children close to Him
   because He loved them so . . .
And with that tenderness of old,
   that same sweet, gentle way,
He holds your little loved one close
   within His arms today . . .
And you'll find comfort in your faith
   that in His home above
The God of little children
   gives your little one His love . . .
So think of your little darling
   lighthearted and happy and free
Playing in God's promised land
   where there is joy eternally.

When a rose climbs over a garden wall, you cannot see it, but you know it is blooming on the other side. So think of your little one as having walked into another room beyond the sight of your vision and the touch of your hand . . . and let your love for her live on by giving it lavishly to all the other little girls and boys.

H.S.R.

For Such a Little While

God gave you your daughter
  for such a little while,
He put a bit of heaven
  in the sunshine of her smile.
He took dust from the brightest twinkling stars
  and made her sparkling eyes,
And now, she's gone back home to God,
  to play up in the skies.
And though she left so quickly
  that your hearts are grieved and sad,
We know she lives with God
  and her small heart is glad.
And though your precious darling
  was just a rosebud small.
She'll bloom in all her beauty
  on the other side of the wall.

Peace I leave with you; my peace I give to you; not as the world gives do I give to you. Let not your hearts be troubled, neither let them be afraid.

John 14:27

The Legend of the Raindrop

The legend of the raindrop
   has a lesson for us all
As it trembled in the heavens
   questioning whether it should fall.
For the glistening raindrop argued
   to the angels of the sky,
"I am beautiful and lovely
   as I sparkle here on high,
And hanging here I will become
   part of the rainbow's hue
And I'll shimmer like a diamond
   for all the world to view."
But the angel told the raindrop,
   "Do not hesitate to go,
For you will be more beautiful
   if you fall to earth below,
For you will sink into the soil
   and be lost awhile from sight,
But when you reappear on earth,
   you'll be looked on with delight.
For you will be the raindrop
   that quenched the thirsty ground
And helped the lovely flowers
   to blossom all around,

And in your resurrection
    you'll appear in queenly clothes
With the beauty of the lily
    and the fragrance of the rose.
Then, when you wilt and wither,
    you'll become part of the earth
And make the soil more fertile
    and give the new flowers birth."
For there is nothing ever lost
    or eternally neglected,
For everything God ever made
    is always resurrected.

I have learned of the tragedy that has torn your heart apart. There's so little words can say to soften your sorrow, for it's so overwhelming that you are lost in the agony and the anguish of its immensity.

But Sunday will be Mother's Day, and I am hoping that through remembrance you will gain strength to realize that the purpose of all living is to die and that death opens the door to the glory of living. I can promise you that your daughter is waiting to welcome you.

I know all these words seem meaningless to you now. I am only going to ask you one thing, and that is to think of the wonderful years you experienced as her mother. In doing this, it will awaken the miracle of her birth. Dwell on this thought and all the joy she brought.

Birth and death in God's hands are still unfathomable mysteries. When she was born into this world, it was God who breathed the breath of life into her. While man has figured out the process of conception and birth, it was God, and God alone, who breathed life into what was physically conceived, and it will always remain the secret that only eternity can unveil.

Why this tragedy should be, we all ask, and we cannot help but wonder how this kind, wonderful God could allow this brutal violence to happen to this lovely, innocent girl.

Violence is the product of man, for God gives us all a choice. It was man himself who changed all God's plans, and now God's children are the innocent victims of sinful mankind.

This does not mean that God is not with them and taking care of them, for our lives are more than a physical journey. It is supposed to be a spiritual experience.

If you recall, it says in the Bible, "They meant it for evil, but God meant it for good!" There are many times when injustice seems to be dominant, and it is only natural to feel God's law of justice is not always at work. But God's law will adjust and regulate all kinds of conditions and situations. So, I'm going to ask you to keep praying without ceasing, and remember whatsoever you ask in prayer, that you will receive if you truly love the Lord and are looking forward to dwelling with Him someday.

H.S.R.

*This is the message we have heard
from him and declare to you: God
is light, in him there is no darkness
at all.*

1 John 1:5 NIV

Death of a
Dear Friend

My dear friend,

I just heard of your sister's swift departure into the promised land of eternity!

It all seems quite unbelievable that this could have happened so suddenly to shatter the whole pattern of your life. But right now you are so shocked and over-whelmed by the unexpectedness of this sudden sorrow that your heart is filled with loneliness and your mind with questioning and despair envelops you.

You are wondering why God let this happen when she, who was in the prime of life, active, and healthy with so much to live for, was chosen instead of your elderly mother to make her pilgrimage into eternity.

Your dear mother has been waiting for the angel of death to take her gently by the hand and lead her across the threshold, releasing her from all pain and suffering. But the ways of God are beyond explaining, and there are so many things in life that we cannot understand, but we must trust God's judgment and be guided by His hand. And He often takes our loved ones unexpectedly to open up new avenues of faith for us, for Christians develop in the time of trouble.

Right now, words will not reach your aching hearts, for there just seems to be nothing anyone can say to soften your sorrow or lessen your loss, which is so new, keen, and sharp with the pain of parting. But I want you to remember that death seems to draw us closer to each other and to God, and somehow heaven does not seem too far away when our loved ones go to live there.

You have a wonderful husband who shares your sorrow and who completely understands your overwhelming sense of loss, grief, and questioning. To know this should help you adjust to the future, where you can put your grief back away from the present and again be the sweet, kind, helpful lady you have always been.

I know life for all of you can never be the same — richer and fuller, but never the same — but your loved one's passing has given your lives a new dimension.

H.S.R.

A Consolation Meditation

On the wings
   of death and sorrow
God sends us
   new hope for tomorrow,
And in His mercy
   and His grace
He gives us strength
   to bravely face
The lonely days
   that stretch ahead
And know our loved one
   is not dead
But only sleeping
   and out of sight
Until we meet in that land
   that is always bright.

When a light goes out of our lives and we are left in darkness and do not know which way to go, we must put our hands into the hand of God and ask Him to lead us. And if we let our lives become a prayer until we are strong enough to stand under the weight of our thoughts again, somehow even the most difficult hours are bearable.

H.S.R.

There Is No Death

There is no night without a dawning,
    no winter without a spring,
And beyond death's dark horizon,
    our hearts once more will sing.
For those who leave us for a while
    have only gone away
Out of a restless, careworn world
    into a brighter day
Where there will be no partings
    and time is not counted by years,
Where there are no trials or troubles,
    no worries, no cares, and no tears.

So do not fear, for I am with you,
do not be dismayed, for I am your God.
Isaiah 41:10 NIV

A Memorial Day Prayer

They served and fought and died
   so that we might be safe and free,
Grant them, O Lord, eternal peace
   and give them the victory!
And in these days of unrest,
   filled with grave uncertainty,
Let's not forget the price they paid
   to keep our country free.
And so, on this Memorial Day,
   we offer up a prayer,
May the people of all nations
   be united in Thy care,
And grant us understanding
   and teach us how to live,
So we may lose our selfish pride
   and learn to love and give.
And keep us ever mindful
   of the fighting men who sleep
In Arlington and foreign lands
   so we may ever keep
The light of freedom burning
   in their honor through the years
And hear their cry for peace on earth
   resounding in our ears.

Forgive us our transgressions
and, God, be with us yet
Lest in our pride and arrogance,
we heedlessly forget.

A Ship Sails Away

A ship sails away,
    and we see it no more,
But we know it is going
    to some other shore.
Our dear ones pass on,
    and we see them no more,
But we know they are waiting
    on some other shore.

You who dwell in the shelter of the Most High, who abide in the shadow of the Almighty, say to the Lord, "My refuge and my fortress; my God, in whom I trust." For he will rescue you from the snare of the fowler, from the destroying pestilence. With his pinions, he will cover you, and under his wings you shall take refuge; his faithfulness is a buckler and a shield. You shall not fear the terror of the night, nor the arrow that flies by day; nor the pestilence that roams in darkness, nor the devastating plague at noon.

Psalm 91:1–6 NAB

A Prayer for Those Lost in Battle

Give eternal rest to them, O Lord,
   whose souls have taken flight,
And lead them to a better world
   where there is peace and light.
Grant them eternal freedom
   from conflict, war, and care,
And fulfill for them Thy prophecy —
   there shall be no night there.

Death is not sent as punishment. It is a graduation to glory! And even though in this instance, death came in a cruel, inhuman way, God had taken their souls before the cruelty of death was even apparent to them. You must realize that they rose unencumbered to meet God, and they are safe and free where all the problems of this restless, violent world will no longer disturb their young minds.

H.S.R.

"Well done, good and faithful servant; you have been faithful over a little, I will set you over much; enter into the joy of your master."

Matthew 25:21

He Restores My Soul

I have some advice to offer you because I know what you are going through.

Each morning when you awaken, read the Twenty-third Psalm. Read it slowly and carefully. Think about each word and phrase and meditate on the assurance of the words. I believe it is one of the, if not the, most powerful pieces of writing in this world.

Concentrate on the following:

1. The Lord is your Shepherd, and He is leading you and anointing your scars with the balm of His love.
2. God is promising to restore your soul, revive your weary body, and to take you into a cool, clear place of rest.
3. No matter how steep the hill or mountain, the Lord is going to climb it with you.

Just writing this note to you, I myself have gained extra strength. Often in my life, I have reached out for the hand of my Shepherd and when I get very quiet, I can feel the very presence of God. Sometimes I even imagine that I am just a little lamb who doesn't know where to go, but I have my Shepherd to lead me and I know He will not let me fall.

He has often brought me through troubled waters and He will bring you safely through, too, no matter which side of life or death is your destination.

Take my suggestion and you will be surprised how calm and wonderful you feel.

My prayers are with you,

H.S.R.

There's Peace and Calm in the Twenty-third Psalm

With the Lord as your shepherd
  you have all that you need
For if you follow in His footsteps
  wherever He may lead,
He will guard and guide and keep you
  in His loving, watchful care,
And when traveling in dark valleys,
  your shepherd will be there.
His goodness is unfailing,
  His kindness knows no end,
For the Lord is a good shepherd
  on whom you can depend.
So when your heart is troubled,
  you'll find quiet peace and calm
If you open up the Bible
  and just read this treasured Psalm.

The Lord is my shepherd, I shall not want; he makes me lie down in green pastures. He leads me besides still waters; he restores my soul.

Psalm 23:1–3

Only the Love of the Lord Endures!

Everything in life is passing,
   and whatever we possess
Cannot endure forever
   but ends in nothingness,
For there are no safety boxes
   nor vaults that can contain
The possessions we collected
   and desire to retain.
So all that man acquires,
   be it power, fame, or jewels,
Is but limited and earthly,
   only treasure made for fools.
For only in God's kingdom
   can man find enduring treasure,
Priceless gifts of love and beauty,
   more than mortal man can measure,
And the riches he accumulates
   he can keep and part with never,
For only in God's kingdom
   do our treasures last forever.
So use the word *forever*
   with sanctity and love,
For nothing is forever
   but the love of God above!

Never Alone

What more can we ask of our Father
   than to know we are never alone,
That His mercy and love
   are unfailing,
And He makes all our
   problems His own.

*The Lord is my light and my salvation; whom shall I fear? The
Lord is the stronghold of my life; of whom shall I be afraid?*

Psalm 27:1

Good Morning, God!

You are ushering in another day
  untouched and freshly new
So here I come to ask You, God,
  if You'll renew me, too.
Forgive the many errors
  that I made yesterday,
And let me try again, dear God
  to walk closer in Thy way.
But, Father, I am well aware
  I can't make it on my own,
So take my hand and hold it tight,
  for I can't walk alone!

*At times like these man is helpless. It is only God who can speak
the words that calm the sea, still the wind, and ease the pain . . .
so lean on Him and you will never walk alone.*

H.S.R.

God's Mighty Handiwork

The earth is the Lord's,
   and the fullness thereof,
It speaks of His greatness,
   and it sings of His love.
It whispers of mysteries
   we cannot comprehend,
Of a beautiful land
   where life has no end.

Now if Christ is preached as raised from the dead, how can some of you say that there is no resurrection of the dead? But if there is no resurrection of the dead, then Christ has not been raised; if Christ has not been raised, then our preaching is in vain and your faith is in vain.

1 Corinthians 15:12–14

Life Is Forever!
Death Is a Dream!

If we did not go to sleep at night,
 we'd never awaken to see the light,
And the joy of watching a new day break
 or meeting the dawn by some quiet lake
Would never be ours unless we slept
 while God and all His angels kept
A vigil through this little death
 that's over with the morning's breath.
And death, too, is a time of sleeping,
 for those who die are in God's keeping,
And there's a sunrise for each soul,
 for life, not death, is God's promised goal.

Whether we are here on earth or the vast unknown above, it simply is impossible to go beyond God's love.

             H.S.R.

Death Opens the Door to Life Evermore

We live a short while on earth below,
   reluctant to die, for we do not know
Just what dark death is all about,
   and so we view it with fear and doubt.
Not certain of what is around the bend,
   we look on death as the final end
To all that made us mortal beings,
   and yet there lies beyond our seeing
A beautiful life so full and complete
   that we should leave with hurrying feet
To walk with God by sacred streams
   amid beauty and peace beyond our dreams.
For all who believe in the risen Lord
   have been assured of this reward,
And death for them is just graduation
   to a higher realm of wide elevation.
For life on earth is a transient affair,
   just a few brief years in which to prepare
For a life that is free from pain and tears,
   where time is not counted by hours or years.
For death is only the method God chose
   to colonize heaven with the souls of those

Who by their apprenticeship on earth
   proved worthy to dwell in
      the land of new birth.
So death is not sad, it's a time for elation,
   a joyous transition, the soul's emigration
Into a place where the soul's safe and free
   to live with God through eternity.

Death Is Only a Part of Life

We enter this world
   from the great unknown,
And God gives each spirit
   a form of its own
And endows this form
   with a heart and a soul
To spur man on
   to his ultimate goal.
For all men are born
   to return as they came,
And birth and death
   are in essence the same,
And man is born
   to die and arise,
For beyond this world
   in beauty there lies
The purpose of death,
   which is but to gain
Life everlasting
   in God's great domain.
And no one needs make
   this journey alone,
For God has promised
   to take care of His own.

On Death's Other Side

While we can't see
  what's on death's other side,
We know that our Father
  will richly provide
All that He promised
  to those who believe,
And His kingdom is waiting
  for us to receive.

We know that we have passed out of death into life, because we love the brethren. He who does not love abides in death.

1 John 3:14

Death Is the Gateway to Eternal Life

Death is just another step
   along life's changing way,
No more than just a gateway
   to a new and better day.
And parting from our loved ones
   is much easier to bear,
When we know that they are waiting
   for us to join them there.
So death is just a natural thing
   like the closing of a door,
As we start upon a journey
   to a new and distant shore,
And none need make this journey
   undirected or alone,
For God promised us safe passage
   to this vast and great unknown.
So let your grief be softened,
   and yield not to despair,
You have only placed your loved one
   in the loving Father's care.

For since we believe that Jesus died and rose again, even so, through Jesus, God will bring with him those who have fallen asleep.

1 Thessalonians 4:14

The next time that you walk along the white, sandy beach of an ocean or along the river bank or lake shore, take time to observe any group of friendly vacationers as some of their members board a fishing or sailing boat and others of the group wait on shore. You see them waving exuberantly to their friends as they cast off. Over the water the boat sails. Watch closely as the boat travels from the shore. Farther and farther it goes. Smaller and smaller it becomes until it is eventually out of sight and over the horizon.

The passengers and the boat are still there but, for a period of time, merely out of the range of a mortal's vision. So it is with the passing of a loved one.

And in the fourth watch of the night he came to them, walking on the sea. But when the disciples saw him walking on the sea, they were terrified, saying, "It is a ghost!" And they cried for fear. But immediately he spoke to them, saying, "Take heart, it is I; have no fear." And Peter answered him, "Lord, if it is you, bid me come to you on the water." He said, "Come." So Peter got out of the boat and walked on the water and came to Jesus; but when he saw the wind, he was afraid, and beginning to sink he cried out, "Lord save me." Jesus immediately reached out his hand and caught him, saying to him, "O man of little faith, why did you doubt?"
Matthew 14:25–31

I call upon the Lord who is worthy to be praised, and I am saved from my enemies.

Psalm 18:3

God's Springtime

How wonderful and mysterious are the workings of the Lord! Nature, with its memorable and poignant messages, is teaching us the lesson of life. The seasons, the flowers, and even the butterflies are telling, in kaleidoscope form, the story of death and resurrection.

Winter, so barren and cold, progresses into spring, warm and flourishing; a dried lily bulb develops into a lovely, fragrant, blooming flower, and a drab, wormlike caterpillar metamorphoses into a colorful and beautiful butterfly! Appreciate the glory, the fascination, the miracle, the hope, the faith, the peace, and the comfort of it all.

But if we have died with Christ, we believe that we shall also live with him. For we know that Christ being raised from the dead will never die again; death no longer has dominion over him.

Romans 6:8–9

All Nature Proclaims Eternal Life

Flowers sleeping 'neath the snow,
  awakening when the spring winds blow;
Leafless trees so bare before,
  gowned in lacy green once more;
Hard, unyielding, frozen sod
  now softly carpeted by God;
Still streams melting in the spring,
  rippling over rocks that sing;
Barren, windswept, lonely hills
  turning gold with daffodils—
These miracles are all around
  within our sight and touch and sound,
As true and wonderful today
  as when the stone was rolled away,
Proclaiming to all doubting men
  that in God all things live again.

God wants us to reap a great spiritual crop from the seeds of suffering and sorrow. Remember, God never makes mistakes and He never plows where He does not intend to sow seeds ... and when He sows spiritual seeds, there is always a crop to fill the storehouse of the soul to overflowing!

H.S.R.

Spring Awakens What Autumn Puts to Sleep

A garden of asters of varying hues,
  crimson-pink and violet-blues,
Blossoming in the hazy fall
  wrapped in autumn's lazy pall —
But early frost stole in one night,
  and like a chilling, killing blight,
It touched each pretty aster's head
  and now the garden's still and dead,
And all the lovely flowers that bloomed
  will soon be buried and entombed
In winter's icy shroud of snow,
  but, oh, how wonderful to know
That after winter comes the spring
  to breathe new life in everything,
And all the flowers that fell in death
  will be awakened by spring's breath.
For in God's plan men, women, and flowers
  can only reach bright, shining hours
By dying first to rise in glory
  and prove again the resurrection story.
Live for Me and die for Me and I, Thy God, will
  set you free!

There's Always a Springtime

After the winter comes the spring
   to show us again that in everything
There's always a renewal divinely planned,
   flawlessly perfect, the work of God's hand.
And just like the seasons that come and go
   when the flowers of spring lay buried in snow,
God sends to the heart in its winter of sadness
   a springtime awakening of new hope
      and gladness,
And loved ones who sleep in a season of death
   will, too, be awakened by God's
      life-giving breath.

After the deep waters recede and the dark hours give way to the light of God's love, you will be able to walk out of the shadows of sadness into the brightness of gladness, for you will realize that the sorrow of today is the joy of tomorrow.

H.S.R.

I Know That
My Redeemer Liveth

They asked me how I know it's true
   that the Savior lived and died
And if I believe the story
   that the Lord was crucified.
And I have so many answers
   to prove His Holy Being,
Answers that are everywhere
   within the realm of seeing.
The leaves that fell at autumn
   and were buried in the sod,
Now budding on the tree boughs
   to lift their arms to God.
The flowers that were covered
   and entombed beneath the snow,
Pushing through the darkness
   to bid the spring hello.
On every side great nature
   retells this miraculous story,
So who am I to question
   the resurrection glory?

All Nature Tells Us Nothing Really Ever Dies

Nothing ever really dies
   that is not born anew,
The miracles of nature
   all tell us this is true.
The flowers sleeping peacefully
   beneath the winter's snow
Awaken from their icy grave
   when spring winds start to blow,
And little brooks and singing streams
   icebound beneath the snow
Begin to babble merrily
   beneath the sun's warm glow.
And all around on every side,
   new life and joy appear
To tell us nothing ever dies
   and we should have no fear,
For death is just a detour
   along life's winding way
That leads God's chosen children
   to a bright and glorious day.

Each Spring, God Renews His Promise

Death is a season that man must pass through
and, just like the flowers, God wakens him, too.
So why should we grieve
when our loved ones die,
for we'll meet them again in a cloudless sky.

Heaven is real. It's a positive place where those who believe meet God face to face.

H.S.R.

In God's Tomorrow There Is Eternal Spring

All nature heeds the call of spring
   as God awakens everything,
And all that seemed so dead and still
   experiences a sudden thrill
As springtime lays a magic hand
   across God's vast and fertile land.
Oh, the joy in standing by
   to watch a sapphire springtime sky
Or see a fragile flower break through
   what just a day ago or two
Seemed barren ground still hard with frost,
   for in God's world, no life is lost,
And flowers sleep beneath the ground,
   but when they hear spring's waking sound,
They push themselves through layers of clay
   to reach the sunlight of God's day.
And man and woman, like flowers, too, must sleep
   until called from the darkened deep
To live in that place where angels sing
   and where there is eternal spring.

I love thee, O Lord, my strength. The Lord is my rock, and my fortress.

Psalm 18:1–2

Because He Lives, We, Too, Shall Live

In this restless world of struggle
　　it is very hard to find
Answers to the questions
　　that daily come to mind.
We cannot see the future,
　　what's beyond is still unknown,
For the secret of God's kingdom
　　still belongs to Him alone.
But He granted us salvation
　　when His Son was crucified,
For life became immortal
　　because our Savior died.

*Life is change but never loss, for Christ purchased
our salvation when He died upon the cross.*

H.S.R.